Truck-Mania!

By Caroline Bingham

Gareth Stevens Publishing
A WORLD ALMANAC EDUCATION GROUP COMPANY

Please visit our web site at: www.garethstevens.com
For a free color catalog describing Gareth Stevens Publishing's list
of high-quality books and multimedia programs, call 1-800-542-2595 (USA)
or 1-800-387-3178 (Canada). Gareth Stevens Publishing's fax: (414) 332-3567.

Library of Congress Cataloging-in-Publication Data

Bingham, Caroline, 1962–
        Truck-mania! / by Caroline Bingham. — North American ed.
            p. cm. — (Vehicle-mania!)
        Includes index.
        Contents: Peterbilt 379 tractor — Mercedes-Benz actros — Mack road train —
    Liebherr LTM 1500 crane — Komatsu 930E dump truck — LeTourneau L-2350 wheel loader —
    Komatsu D575A super dozer — Caterpillar 385L excavator — Oshkosh S-Series mixer truck —
    JCB backhoe loader — Mercedes-Benz tow truck — Oshkosh snow mover — John Deere 9750 combine.
        ISBN 0-8368-3785-1 (lib. bdg.)
        1. Trucks—Juvenile literature. [1. Trucks.] I. Title. II. Series.
    TL230.15.B53625 2003
    629.224—dc21   2003043917

This North American edition first published in 2004 by
Gareth Stevens Publishing
A WRC Media Company
330 West Olive Street, Suite 100
Milwaukee, Wisconsin 53212

This U.S. edition copyright © 2004 by Gareth Stevens Inc.
Original edition copyright © 2003 ticktock Entertainment Ltd.
First published in Great Britain in 2003 by ticktock Media Ltd.,
Unit 2, Orchard Business Centre, North Farm Road, Tunbridge Wells,
Kent, TN2 3XF, United Kingdom.

We would like to thank: Jamie Asher, Peter Symons at Ice Marketing,
and Elizabeth Wiggans.

Gareth Stevens Editor: Jim Mezzanotte
Gareth Stevens Art Direction: Tammy West

Photo credits: Ainscough Crane Hire:
3br, 10-11, 31tl; Alvey & Towers: 4-5c, 6-7c,
24-25; Caterpillar: 18-19c; Construction
Photo Library: 19t; Corbis: 3bl, 8-9;
JCB: 2, 22-23, 32br and OFC; John Deere: 28-29;
Komatsu: 12-13, 16-17; Letourneau Inc: 14-15c;
Peterbilt: 4; Mack Trucks: 8; Oshkosh: 20-21, 26-27.

Printed in the United States of America

2 3 4 5 6 7 8 9 09 08 07 06 05

CONTENTS

PETERBILT 379 TRACTOR

Tractor-trailers transport all kinds of **cargo** and often travel long distances. A tractor-trailer has two parts — a large truck called a **tractor** and a long trailer that connects to the back of the tractor. Peterbilt is an American company that makes tractors. The 379 is one of Peterbilt's most popular models.

Peterbilt has been selling trucks since 1939. Peterbilt trucks are famous for their performance, comfort, and reliability.

The truck's huge engine sits inside the long hood, which is made of **aluminum**.

The whole hood tips forward to allow easy access to the Peterbilt 379's powerful engine.

Did You Know?

Many tractors have sleeping compartments so the driver has a place to rest during long trips.

MERCEDES-BENZ ACTROS

A cabover truck has a **cab** located above the engine. It is shorter than a truck that has the cab behind the engine. Cabover trucks are often used in countries where longer trucks are not allowed. The Actros is built by Mercedes-Benz, a German company that also makes cars.

Wind can slow a truck down and cause it to use more fuel. The Actros has **spoilers** on the roof to limit the effect of the wind.

Did You Know?

Actros trucks have transported everything from dairy products to racing cars.

Actros trucks often travel long distances, so Mercedes-Benz makes them very comfortable for drivers. The cabs are **soundproofed** to keep out engine noise.

FACTS AND STATS

First Model Year: 1996

Origin: Germany

Length: 59 feet (18 m)

Width: 7.9 feet (2.4 m)

Height: 11.5 feet (3.5 m)

Weight: 16.5 tons (15 m tons)

Wheelbase: 12.8 feet (3.9 m)

Fuel Capacity:
159 gallons to 186 gallons
(600 l to 705 l)

Maximum Load:
32 tons (29 m tons)

Maximum Power: 460 hp

Maximum Speed: 120 miles
(193 km) per hour

This Actros is a tractor, so it connects to a **semitrailer**. A semitrailer only has wheels in the back. The front of the trailer sits over the tractor's rear wheels.

MACK ROAD TRAIN

Have you ever heard the saying, "built like a Mack truck?" Mack trucks are strong and reliable. In Australia, Mack tractors pull three or more trailers at a time. These "road trains" haul huge loads between cities. Mack trucks were first made in the United States, but now they are also made in other countries.

All Mack trucks have a tiny metal bulldog on the hood. The most powerful Mack model has a gold bulldog. All the other Mack models have silver bulldogs.

Mack tractors that pull road trains in Australia have very powerful engines. Since the weather in Australia can get very hot, the tractors also have huge radiators to keep the engines cool.

Did You Know?

People who buy Mack trucks can have the trucks built exactly how they want them. Buyers can choose everything, from engine size to the right kind of sleeping compartment.

FACTS AND STATS

First Model Year: 1977

Origin: Australia

Length: 174 feet (53 m)

Width: 13 feet (4 m)

Height: 11.5 feet (3.5 m)

Weight: 15.4 tons (14 m tons)

Wheelbase:
17.3 feet to 20. 3 feet
(5.3 m to 6.2 m)

Fuel Capacity:
400 gallons (1,530 l)

Maximum Load:
264 tons (240 m tons)

Maximum Power: 600 hp

Maximum Speed:
60 miles (97 km) per hour

A Mack tractor pulling a road train has large fuel tanks, so it can travel long distances before stopping to refuel.

LIEBHERR LTM 1500 CRANE

The Liebherr LTM 1500 is a huge crane that can be driven from place to place. The long jib, or arm, can be extended like a radio's antenna. This crane can lift a load that equals the weight of five hundred cars!

Four **outriggers** help keep the crane steady while it is lifting. When the outriggers are fully extended, the crane is almost 33 feet (10 m) wide.

Did You Know?

The largest cranes in the world can lift 880 tons (800 m tons) — about the weight of six fully grown blue whales!

FACTS AND STATS

First Model Year: 2002

Origin: Germany

Length: 70.8 feet (21.6 m)

Width: 9.8 feet (3 m)

Height: 13 feet (4 m)

Weight:
138 tons (125 m tons)

Fuel Capacity:
158 gallons (600 l)

Maximum Load:
551 tons (500 m tons)

**Maximum Power
(Drive Engine):** 598 hp
(Lifting Engine): 326 hp

Maximum Speed:
50 miles (80 km) per hour

To lift loads, large cranes use heavy lifting blocks that have big hooks. A lifting block can weigh more than a car.

The crane's jib can extend to a length of 275 feet (84 m). An extra jib can also be added to the main jib, bringing the total length to an amazing 574 feet (175 m).

KOMATSU 930E DUMP TRUCK

The Komatsu 930E dump truck is so huge that it is not allowed to travel on roads. When the truck moves to a new work site, it must be taken apart and transported in pieces. This truck works in **quarries** and mines, where it is used to move enormous loads of rock, earth, and coal.

Did You Know?

The driver's seat is almost 16 feet (5 m) above the ground. To get to it, the driver uses a set of stairs!

This truck has a huge steel container that could hold six full-size cars. **Pistons** tilt the container up so the load slides out.

The dump truck's engine is heavier than the load it carries, so the truck will not tip over as the container lifts.

Dump trucks such as the 930E have large fuel tanks. The trucks often run all day long, and they guzzle huge amounts of fuel.

LETOURNEAU L-2350 WHEEL LOADER

The LeTourneau L-2350 wheel loader is the biggest loader in the world. At mining sites, it helps move huge piles of earth and rock by carrying the loads to dump trucks. You could park a large car in the bucket of this massive machine!

In about 25 seconds, the L-2350 can pick up and drop off a load. Its bucket reaches more than 23 feet (7 m) into the air.

Did You Know?

Inside the cab of the L-2350, the driver steers the truck and operates the bucket by moving a joystick.

The L-2350 has the largest mining tires ever made. Each tire is almost 13 feet (4 m) tall and weighs almost 9 tons (8 m tons).

A wheel loader has a lot of its weight low to the ground, so the machine will not tip over when operating on a hill.

FACTS AND STATS

First Model Year: 2001

Origin: United States

Length (Bucket Down):
64.6 feet (19.7 m)

Bucket Width: 22.3 feet (6.8 m)

Height (Bucket Raised):
43.6 feet (13.3 m)

Weight:
209 tons (190 m tons)

Fuel Capacity:
1,050 gallons (3,975 l)

Bucket Capacity:
1,429.7 cubic feet
(40.5 cubic meters)

Maximum Load:
79 tons (72 m tons)

Maximum Power: 2,300 hp

Maximum Speed:
10.5 miles (16.9 km) per hour

KOMATSU D575A SUPER DOZER

Did You Know?

A bulldozer is also called a tractor, blade, or dozer.

When heavy earth and rock need to be pushed out of the way, a bulldozer is the machine for the job. The Komatsu D575A Super Dozer is the world's largest bulldozer, and it has a huge **blade**. Over forty Super Dozers are now at work in mines and quarries around the world.

The Super Dozer uses **tracks** instead of wheels. Tracks are flexible metal bands that turn. They dig into the earth to roll easily on uneven ground.

The Super Ripper attachment can tear up 2,204 tons (2,000 m tons) of earth every hour. It has teeth that are over 3 feet (1 m) long!

FACTS AND STATS

First Model Year: 1991

Origin: Japan

Length:
49.2 feet (15 m)

Blade Width:
24.6 feet (7.5 m)

Blade Height:
10.7 feet (3.25 m)

Weight:
84.3 tons (76.5 m tons)

Fuel Capacity:
555 gallons (2,100 l)

Maximum Load:
31.4 tons (28.5 m tons)

Maximum Power: 1,150 hp

Maximum Speed
7.5 miles (12 km) per hour

KOMATSU

D575A

Super Dozer

This dozer is more than twice as big as any other large dozer now being made.

CATERPILLAR 385L EXCAVATOR

Excavators are digging machines. A bucket with teeth scoops up the earth and drops it into a dump truck. Caterpillar builds excavators of many different sizes, including the giant 385L. This machine digs huge amounts of dirt very quickly.

Did You Know?

Since the 1930s, excavators and other construction machines have usually been painted bright yellow. This color is easy for drivers to see when the machines are working on roads and highways, and it is sometimes called "highway yellow."

The boom is the curved arm attached to the body. The dipper is a second arm attached to the end of the boom. The bucket attaches to the end of the dipper.

The body of the 385L can turn all the way around even while the tracks stay in one place.

The whole machine turns when one track stops and the other track keeps going.

OSHKOSH S-SERIES MIXER TRUCK

The Oshkosh S-Series mixer truck is a huge machine. It carries massive amounts of sand, gravel, and **cement** in a large container called a drum. As the truck travels to a construction site, water is added to the drum, which turns slowly to mix everything into **concrete**.

This truck has a chute in front for pouring out concrete. The chute can be moved in almost any direction.

After the drum is emptied, it is flushed out with water to get rid of leftover cement. If the cement dried, the truck would be ruined!

FACTS AND STATS

First Model Year: 1999

Origin: United States

Length: 40 feet (12.2 m)

Width: 13 feet (4 m)

Height: 14 feet (4.3 m)

Weight:
60.6 tons (55 m tons)

Fuel Capacity:
50 gallons (190 l)

Water Capacity:
150 gallons (568 l)

Maximum Load:
356.5 cubic feet
(10.1 cubic m)

Maximum Power: 335 hp

Maximum Speed:
50 miles (80 km) per hour

When the drum turns in one direction, all the materials are mixed together. When it turns in the other direction, the concrete gets pushed out.

JCB BACKHOE LOADER

A backhoe loader can do many different jobs. It has a small bucket in back for digging, like an excavator, and it has a large shovel in front for moving loads, like a wheel loader. The British company JCB makes backhoe loaders that are used all over the world.

Did You Know?

A backhoe loader is very similar to a farm tractor but has special attachments for digging and for moving soil, rocks, and other materials.

People who buy JCB backhoe loaders can customize their machines. They can choose the size of the bucket and the length of the arm.

JCB puts on shows featuring the Dancing Diggers. This team of five backhoe loaders and two mini excavators performs a variety of stunts.

FACTS and STATS

First Model Year: 1962

Origin: Britain

Length:
18.3 feet (5.6 m)

Width: 7.9 feet (2.4 m)

Shovel Width:
7.9 feet (2.4 m)

Height: 11.8 feet (3.6 m)

Weight:
8.3 tons (7.5 m tons)

Fuel Capacity:
42 gallons (160 l)

Maximum Load:
38.8 cubic feet (1.1 cubic m)

Maximum Dig Depth:
15.4 feet (4.7 m)

Maximum Power: 92 hp

Maximum Speed:
67 miles (108 km) per hour

The bucket swings around to either side of the backhoe loader so the machine does not have to be moved while digging.

MERCEDES-BENZ TOW TRUCK

Did You Know?

Some large tow trucks have **winches** that are powerful enough to pull a barge down a river.

If a truck breaks down or has an accident, a Mercedes-Benz tow truck can take it to a garage for repairs. This large truck is very powerful. It can tow vehicles weighing more than three times its own weight!

Many tow trucks have powerful lights because they are often needed for rescuing vehicles at night.

WILLTHORN-15

KINGS LYNN, NORFOLK · SUFFO
FREEPHONE 0800

CAR & COMMERCIAL RECOVERY SPECIALISTS

TEARS
RECOVERY

RECOVERY

This tow truck was built for a specific job — to tow tanks. It has a huge engine and is made of very strong materials.

The tow truck has a strong metal shelf in back that slides beneath the truck being towed. A winch pulls the vehicle up onto the tow truck.

OSHKOSH SNOW MOVER

When a snowstorm hits, the Oshkosh HB-Series snow mover goes to work. This powerful machine helps keep roads open to traffic by breaking snowdrifts into loose powder and blowing the powder off the road. It is one of the best snow movers in the world.

Able to move 5,510 tons (5,000 m tons) of snow per hour, the Oshkosh HB-Series is the ultimate snow-mover machine.

This machine has two engines. One engine drives the wheels. The other engine powers the blower, which blasts snow off the road.

Did You Know?

The HB-Series snow mover can use many attachments, including sweepers, blowers, and plows.

FACTS AND STATS

First Model Year: 1991

Origin: United States

Length: 27.9 feet (8.5 m)

Width: 4.9 feet (1.5 m)

Height: 11.5 feet (3.5 m)

Weight:
22.5 tons (20.4 m tons)

Fuel Capacity:
250 gallons (946 l)

**Maximum Power
(Drive Engine):** 505 hp

**Maximum Power
(Blower Engine):** 650 hp

Maximum Speed:
45 miles (72 km) per hour

This snow mover has **four-wheel drive.** With this system, the machine can be driven on extremely slippery surfaces.

JOHN DEERE 9750 COMBINE

In the 1800s, ten workers had to work all day to cut down a small field of wheat by hand, and more workers were needed to collect the wheat and **thresh** it to remove the **grain**. Today, a John Deere 9750 combine harvester does the whole process in an hour.

Once the crop has been cut, collected, and threshed, the grain is stored in a tank behind the cab. The straw, or leftover stalks, is collected later.

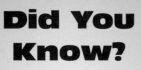

Did You Know?

When the tank of grain is full, it can be emptied into a waiting truck in just a few minutes.

The American firm Deere & Company was founded by a blacksmith named John Deere, who created a very successful plow in the 1830s. The company now makes many kinds of farm machinery.

FACTS AND STATS

First Model Year 1999

Origin: United States

Length: 32.8 feet (10 m)

Width: 19.7 feet (6 m)

Height: 16.4 feet (5 m)

Weight:
22.5 tons (20.4 m tons)

Fuel Capacity: 20,412 kg

Maximum Load:
2,794 gallons (10,572 l)
of grain

Maximum Power: 325 hp

Maximum Speed:
20 miles (32 km) per hour

The harvester has cutting blades in front. The blades are on a rotating wheel that is 19.7 feet (6 m) wide.

GLOSSARY

aluminum: a lightweight metal that is often used in the construction of vehicles.

blade: the attachment at the front of a bulldozer, used to push materials.

cab: the part of a truck or other vehicle where the driver sits.

cargo: a shipment that a vehicle carries from one place to another.

cement: a powder that becomes hard and holds other materials together after water has been added and it has dried.

concrete: a mixture of sand, gravel, cement, and water that is very strong after it dries and is often used in the construction of buildings and other structures.

four-wheel drive: a system that uses an engine's power to drive all four wheels of a vehicle.

grain: the seeds of wheat or other food grasses.

horsepower: a unit of measurement for an engine's power that was originally based on the pulling strength of one horse.

joystick: a lever that can be used to control the direction of a vehicle and the movement of the vehicle's different attachments.

outriggers: long metal bars sticking out from the sides of a construction machine, such as a crane, with feet that rest on the ground to keep the vehicle from tipping over.

pistons: metal tubes that slide in and out of larger metal tubes to move part of a vehicle, such as a dump truck's container, an excavator's bucket, or a bulldozer's blade.

quarries: work sites where stone is taken out of the ground.

radiators: Equipment that keeps an engine from getting too hot by cooling the liquid that flows around the engine's cylinders.

semitrailer: a long trailer with no front wheels that is pulled by a tractor and is used to haul cargo; the rear part of a tractor-trailer.

soundproofed: made of special materials added to keep out noise.

spoilers: attachments to a vehicle's body that help the vehicle cut smoothly through the air and stay steady on the road.

thresh: remove the grain from the stalk of a plant.

tracks: wide, flexible bands, made of many metal bars, that can roll over ground that may be too rough for regular wheels.

tractor: a large, powerful truck, usually with two sets of rear wheels, that is used to pull semitrailers; the front part of a tractor-trailer.

winches: machines that pull or lift objects by winding a cable or rope around a rotating wheel.

INDEX